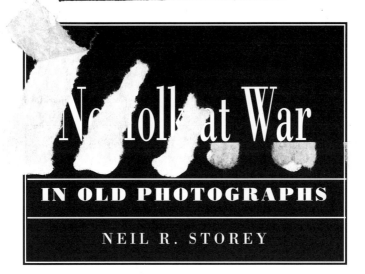

Norfolk at War

IN OLD PHOTOGRAPHS

NEIL R. STOREY

Sutton Publishing Limited
Phoenix Mill · Thrupp · Stroud
Gloucestershire · GL5 2BU

First published 1995

This edition first published in 2002 by
Lucas Books

Copyright © Neil R. Storey, 1995

British Library Cataloguing in Publication Data.
A catalogue record for this book is available from
the British Library.

ISBN 1-90379-710-1

Typeset in 9/10 Sabon.
Typesetting and origination by
Sutton Publishing Limited.
Printed in Great Britain by
J. H. Haynes & Co. Ltd, Sparkford.

This book is dedicated to my grandparents
(who are pictured below)

Mrs Kay Storey, St John Ambulance Women's Section, North Walsham.

Gnr. George Storey, 28th Field Regiment, Royal Artillery, 14th Army, India and Burma.

Contents

The Cromer 'Fencibles', Volunteer Militia, drill on The Marrams, 1798. Ready to combat any threatened invasion by Napoleon, two armed soldiers were even positioned on top of the church tower in case invaders flew over in balloons!

Foreword

One curious feature of today's fast-changing world is the growing interest we all share in the history of events to which we can relate, whether it concerns our own county, family or, in the instance of this admirable book, the impact of successive calls to arms. Neil Storey, in subscribing to the famous Chinese proverb that 'a picture is worth a thousand words', has given us an enjoyable opportunity to gratify our curiosity and be reminded of the challenges and privations faced by our courageous forebears. It is full of interesting information: I for one had no idea that the citizens of Sheringham were subjected to a bombing attack from Zeppelins in 1915. The pictures and narrative are of exceptional quality and interest.

There will be faces recognized and anecdotes recalled. Above all, I'm sure, this book will kindle sentimental memories and remind us of our debt to those who gave so much, and often their lives, so that we who remain could enjoy the fruits of that freedom which should never be taken for granted.

Timothy Colman
Her Majesty's Lord Lieutenant of Norfolk

The Norfolk Recruit's Farewell

In swarms they came, our gallant men,
From Norwich's crowded wards,
From scattered homesteads in the Fen
High Norfolk and the Broads.

From Cromer's Beach to Waveney's Reach
From Yarmouth, Lynn they flock,
From Dereham, Downham, Fakenham,
The good old Norfolk stock.

And thousands more already gone,
You may say – everywhere,
For if there's any fighting on,
The Norfolk man is there.

Cloudesley Brereton

Introduction

Whenever there has been direct aggression against Great Britain, Norfolk has been one of the counties under major threat of invasion and attack. The deep waters and easily accessible landscape surrounding the county are ideal for any prospective raiders. Consequently, since the first locals gathered themselves into armed bands to defend their homes against unknown odds, the unique fighting spirit of Norfolk has been inborn. Traditionally defending what they believe to be right and fighting what they reason to be wrong, Norfolk men and women have never been afraid to stand up for themselves; indeed, their fighting quality has been legendary since the days of Boudicca and the warrior race of the Iceni. In 1381, during the Peasants' Revolt, rebels from all over the county rose up, led by John Litester, the self-styled 'King of the Commons', to fight against the new poll tax and the oppressive laws of the lords and gentry. In 1549, when enclosures of common lands meant that peasants lost much of their grazing rights, fences were sporadically destroyed. These events came to the boil at Wymondham and riots broke out. Robert Kett took charge and organized a march on Norwich, recruiting hoards of angry peasants as they proceeded. Although both these insurrections were put down, the fighting spirit of the county could never be destroyed. Consequently, it is not surprising that when companies of militia were raised country folk were quick to join them. Often raised and funded by parishes, their headquarters and store of armour were in the local church. Later, larger well-organized companies were raised by landed gentry and as time went on, with backing from the Crown and State, they became regiments of the line, such as His Majesty's 9th (East

Norfolk) Regiment of Foot and eventually the Norfolk Regiment – one of the finest regiments ever to be part of the British Army.

Norfolk at War traces the military presence in the county and shows how the people of Norfolk responded when their country was in need, from the days when the Great Yarmouth batteries kept a watchful eye over the North Sea for invaders (1860s to '70s) to when the 1st Battalion of the Royal Norfolks returned from Korea in 1953.

It seems that from the early days of photography the spectacle of the military has attracted the lens. It is also inevitable that when the country is in need the military and emergency services will be caught on film or plate. Although there were restrictions on photography, especially during the Second World War, cameras officially or unofficially would risk 'one for the record'. Consequently many of the photographs in this book have never been published before. Some of the pictures come from the most unlikely sources, and have been collected by the author over the past fourteen years. I have also drawn on many of the interesting photographs I have seen over the years, often tucked away in museum and newspaper records. I have explored many and varied channels, tracking down 'just one more photograph', and everybody I have had the pleasure in meeting during my collecting and research has been more than helpful, laying what they have at my disposal and often pointing me in the direction of yet more interesting pictures and stories. One of the greatest rewards, after painstaking research, is to discover the background to a picture which has no information attached. That moment is indescribable – the picture lives again!

This book is a tribute to all Norfolk people who in any capacity answered the call of their county and country in times of need. Recorded together for the first time in one volume are events such as the coronation salute for King George V, Armistice Day, the first Norwich Poppy Day and VE Day. Also recalled are the great mobilization of the First World War, the Zeppelin attacks and the blitz on the county. Even military and civil organizations as diverse as the Watts' Naval Training School, The Royal Norfolk Veterans Association, and Civil Defence are remembered.

I am not writing this book to glorify war. My family go back hundreds of years in Norfolk and generations have, like so many, answered the call of King or Queen and Country. We all hope and pray there will never be another war on any scale but we must never forget or prejudice those who died, those who returned or those still suffering the effects of man's inhumanity to man. I hope this book provides a fitting record of this county's role in our national military heritage.

Neil R. Storey, 1995

The Early Years

Colour Sgt. James Francis of Cromer, a member of the 3rd Battalion, Norfolk Rifle Volunteers, 1880.

The gateway to Britannia Barracks on Mousehold Heath, c. 1879. The barracks were once home to The Norfolk Regiment, and many would-be soldiers passed through this archway. The view overlooks the fine city of Norwich.

South Star Battery artillerymen, Great Yarmouth, c. 1879. These gunners are members of the Prince of Wales' Own Norfolk Artillery Militia. This noble title was granted on 30 September 1875 by their Honorary Colonel, the Prince of Wales, later to become King Edward VII. They are photographed with one of the 80-pounder guns guarding the deep waters of the North Sea at Yarmouth. Sited on the North and South Denes, the gun batteries were built in the shape of a pentagon and were thus known as star batteries.

Edward, Prince of Wales, poses with his officers after reviewing his artillery militia at their barracks, Southtown, Great Yarmouth, June 1882.

Prince of Wales' Own Norfolk Artillery Band at the Winter Gardens, Great Yarmouth, *c.* 1897. With several regimental depots in the town, residents and visitors were never short of a military band for entertainment at the turn of the century. The roots and noble traditions of the artillery bands can be traced back to 1762, when the Royal Artillery band was formed. It consisted of two trumpets, two horns, two bassoons and four oboes or clarinets.

The 1st Norfolk Royal Garrison Artillery Band, *c.* 1899. By the end of the nineteenth century British regimental bands led the world. Bandmasters had to pass a diploma at Kneller Hall, and their bands played military classics, drawing on great composers and popular music for concert performances.

Men of A (Harleston) Company, 4th Volunteer Battalion, the Norfolk Regiment, proudly march through Harleston under the command of Capt. George Durrant. They are led by the 1st Norfolk Royal Garrison Artillery Band and are on their way to Easter camp and manoeuvres, which spread over twenty-seven days from April to May 1896.

NOTICE

SOUTH DENES.

VOLUNTEER

ENCAMPMENT

The Norfolk Volunteers will be encamped on the South Denes, from the 22nd to the 31st of the present month, and the Worshipful the Mayor suggests that Fishing Boat Owners should not spread their nets on the South Denes, during that time.

BY ORDER,

T. M. BAKER,

TOWN CLERK'S OFFICES, *July 15th*, 1880.
GREAT YARMOUTH.

Town Clerk.

COOPER & SON, STEAM PRINTERS, YARMOUTH.

A poster with a timely warning for fishermen not to catch more than they bargained for when the 4th Volunteer Battalion, The Norfolk Regiment, encamped on the South Denes, Great Yarmouth, July 1880.

Men of the 2nd Volunteer Battalion, The Norfolk Regiment, fire a volley in Norwich market-place as part of the formal celebrations to mark Queen Victoria's Diamond Jubilee, 1897.

Men of 1st (Norwich City) Section, 1st Volunteer Battalion, The Norfolk Regiment, before proceeding to South Africa, 1900.

Men of 3rd Section, the Great Yarmouth Volunteers, 1st Volunteer Service Company, The Norfolk Regiment, after their return from South Africa in 1902.

Four notable Norfolk veterans, 1902. Left to right: PO Robert Skoyles, late Royal Navy, who was the oldest Norfolk veteran, having served in the second Kaffir War, 1846–7; Pte. Robert Nicholls, late Royal Marine Light Infantry, who was awarded the Baltic, Crimean, Turkish Crimean, China and New Zealand medals for campaigns between 1854 and 1866; James 'Old Balaclava' Olley, late 4th Light Dragoons, who was the last Norfolk survivor of the Charge of the Light Brigade, in which he was wounded five times and lost the sight of his left eye. He always wore his Crimean War medals with great pride and maintained that 'Charging the Russian guns we ripp'd thro' 'em like tissue paper!'; Pte. William James, late 93rd Highlanders, who was one of the immortal 'Thin Red Line'. On 25 October 1854, standing just two deep, barely 1,500 men repulsed an attack from a Russian force, estimated to be 25,000 strong, and drove them to full retreat.

The Royal Norfolk Veterans Association, 1902. Following an Old Soldiers' Dinner in autumn 1896 Capt. A.M. Atthill (seated, centre) called a meeting of two hundred veterans, with a view to forming an association. In December 1898 it was founded with a five-point charter, the most important aim being 'To rescue from the workhouse or pauper's grave any old soldier, sailor or marine who through no fault of his own is reduced to destitution.' The good work was rewarded in May 1902, when the title 'Royal' was conferred on the association by King Edward VII.

The unveiling of the Norfolk War Memorial, Norwich, a little after 2.30 p.m., 17 November 1904. Bandmaster E. Elford raises his baton for the band of the 2nd Battalion, Norfolk Regiment, to play the national anthem as Maj.-Gen. A.S. Wynne CB releases the Union Jacks covering the panels of the monument. These panels bear the names of 310 officers, non-commissioned officers and men who had served and died in a Norfolk corps or regiment during the South African War, 1899–1902.

A medals presentation during Sunday church parade for the 1st Norfolk Royal Garrison Artillery (Volunteers), Norwich, 1904. Col. Pook VD awards 2047 Gnr. Edward Mills the Volunteer Force Long Service and Good Conduct medal. This award was for twenty years' service in the volunteer forces, and the character and conduct of the recipient also had to have been 'uniformly good'.

Men of the 3rd Norfolk Volunteers stand proudly by their 'ambulance', for the Sedgeford May Day Carnival, 1906.

Col. H.A. Barclay CVO, TD, ADC in drill order in front of Felbrigg Hall as a lieutenant-colonel holding the MVO, having recently received the Insignia of Commander of the Order of St Olaf from King Haakon while on the Royal Review at Sandringham. In 1901 it was Col. Barclay's task to establish a regiment of yeomanry in Norfolk, a task in which King Edward VII himself took an interest. Squadrons were allotted areas of Norfolk. Recruiting was brisk and on 20 September 1901 over two hundred officers, NCOs and men paraded on foot in civilian clothes on Holkham cricket ground. The regiment went from strength to strength, becoming a unit with a reputation for magnificent turnout and drill. Barclay retired on 6 September 1913 as Colonel of the Regiment, having built the King's Own Royal Regiment Norfolk Imperial Yeomanry.

The annual training camp for the King's Own Royal Regiment Norfolk Imperial Yeomanry was held at Northrepps Hall Park, near Cromer, in 1905. The men are seen here in dismounted review order, being inspected by Lt.-Col. Barclay MVO, Gen. Lord Methuen KCVO and Col. T.O.W. Champion de Crespigny, Inspecting Officer of Imperial Yeomanry, who both expressed themselves absolutely satisfied with the efficient state of the regiment.

The 1908 camp at Sheringham, with the Kings' Own Royal Regiment Norfolk Imperial Yeomanry as part of the new Territorial Force. The Norfolk Yeomanry are brigaded together with the Loyal Suffolk Hussars and the Essex Yeomanry as the Eastern Mounted Brigade. This fine spectacle is their dismounted review order at a Sunday morning church parade, a striking vision of dark blue serge, polished brass and gilt, black helmets and brilliant yellow plumes.

This historic photograph shows the newly launched HMS *Dreadnought* with attendant cruisers and destroyers just off Gorleston Harbour, 1906. A Norfolk man, Adm. Lord Sir John Fisher of Kilverstone was largely responsible for the revolutionary ship. It was the first all big gun, turbine-driven battleship, and made all other existing battleships obsolete. Henceforward all surface navies would be measured by their dreadnought strength.

Sea Cadets and Cadet Norfolk Artillery on parade aboard the training ship *Lord Nelson* near Bishop Bridge, Norwich. Originally the Lowestoft sailing trawler *Elsie*, she was purchased on 24 June 1912 and dedicated to teaching boys good seamanship.

King Edward VII leaves the Chapel Field Drill Hall, where he reviewed the recently formed Territorial Force during his visit to Norwich on 25 October 1909.

Soldiers of the Essex Regiment march past King's Lynn Guildhall as part of the memorial parade following the death of King Edward VII, May 1910.

Men and band boys of the 1st Volunteer Battalion, The Norfolk Regiment, in front of the now-demolished Drill Hall on Chapel Field Gardens, Norwich, 1909.

Crown Point, Trowse, near Norwich, was much used at the turn of the century for military training, especially by the local Territorial Force units such as Royal Engineers, Norfolk Yeomanry and The Norfolk Regiment. Seen here are some officers of the 1st East Anglian Brigade Royal Field Artillery on weekend camp, 1909.

Troopers of the XIIth Prince of Wales' Royal Lancers 'pig-sticking' on Mousehold Heath, Norwich, 1910.

Cavalry Barracks, Norwich, *c*. 1909. Regiments with such wonderful titles as the Norfolk Fencible Cavalry, the Norfolk Rangers and the Norfolk Light Horse Volunteers existed during the nineteenth century or earlier, indicating that Norfolk has had a long cavalry and yeomanry tradition. From 1791, when the Cavalry Barracks were built on the site of an old manor-house, mounted regiments of every description were housed there, from Brunswick Hussars ('Black Brunswickers') of the King's German Legion to 24th Light Dragoons, raised entirely in Norfolk. Often the resident cavalry would be called out to quell public insurrection or even mobilize against threatened invasion!

Produced by the Pioneer Photographic Company for the XIIth (Prince of Wales' Own) Royal Lancers, this Christmas card depicts some of the aspects of cavalry life, from Sunday music at the barracks to the magnificent spectacle of church parade at the cathedral.

A funeral with cavalry honours, Norwich, *c.* 1909. One thing immediately noticeable about all the cavalry stationed in Norwich is the magnificent and unique dress uniform of each regiment. This striking spectacle is the full honours given at the funeral of a cavalryman from the XIIth (Prince of Wales' Own) Royal Lancers. Hats are removed and people stand as the cortège passes over Bishop Bridge on to Riverside Road.

5th (Territorial) Battalion, The Essex Regiment, gathered in their dress blues for Sunday Service at Thetford Camp, June 1911. The padre is standing behind an altar of drums, but unfortunately his congregation seem more interested in the photographer!

Norfolk Yeomanry camp, Crown Point, 1910. This picture graphically shows the changes in warfare during this period: when the swords have been inspected they are replaced in their scabbard and laid on the ground behind, and then the men pick up their SMLE rifles. The uniform has changed dramatically from the wonderful sight of dark blue serge, gilt and yellow plumes to khaki service dress. The Norfolk Yeomanry was never to battle on horseback; it was sent to the hell of Gallipoli, Egypt, Palestine and the Western Front as dismounted yeomanry.

Saluting the coronation of King George V on 22 June 1911. The Norwich festivities opened in front of Britannia Barracks, and a massive crowd gathered on Mousehold Heath to watch a 21-gun salute from the field guns of the 1st East Anglian Brigade Royal Field Artillery.

The band of 4th Battalion, The Norfolk Regiment, proudly marches down London Street on the occasion of King George V's first official visit to Norwich, 28 June 1911.

Norwich Salvation Army citadel workers and members of the Territorial Royal Army Medical Corps, August 1912. They gave care, shelter and food to the hundreds made homeless by the great flood.

Soldiers of the 2nd Battalion, Grenadier Guards, rest in Swaffham market-place during the military manoeuvres of 1912.

A mounted officer of the 2nd Battalion, Coldstream Guards, leads his men along the road from Swaffham, 1912. This was also part of the manoeuvres, which were some of the largest ever seen in Norfolk. Almost every section of the British Army took part and the exercises were based on the 'red' army invading and the 'yellow' army defending.

Men of the 1st East Anglian Brigade (Territorial), Royal Field Artillery, cross the Wensum on a pontoon as part of one of their Field Days, 1913. Wives and sweethearts watch the display. Nobody could have dreamed of what was to happen the following year.

SECTION TWO

The First World War

L.-Cpl. Ernest Hawes, aged nineteen. The son of Daniel and Georgina Hawes of Lakenham, he was killed in action while serving with the 8th (Service) Battalion, The Norfolk Regiment, on 16 October 1915. He is buried in Norfolk Cemetery, on the Somme Front, east of Albert. He was one of almost twelve thousand Norfolk men and women killed during the Great War.

War was declared at 11.00 p.m. on Tuesday 4 August 1914. The next day the companies of the 5th (Territorial) Battalion, The Norfolk Regiment, poured into East Dereham market-place, ready to proceed to their war stations.

At Artillery Barracks, All Saints Green, Norwich, the territorials of the 1st East Anglian Brigade, Royal Field Artillery are mobilized for war, 1914. The posters call out for volunteers to 'Come and join our happy throng'; the recruiting drive was on. Many expected the war to be over by Christmas. None of these boys could have known what was to come, or comprehended the horrors of the new warfare. I cannot but wonder how few came back.

The first Norfolk contingent of the British Expeditionary Force (BEF) leaves Thorpe station, Norwich. These are just a few of the 110,000 men who proceeded to France and fought in the Marne, Ypres and Mons under Field Marshal Sir John French. In the words of Lawrence Binyon's poem, 'For The Fallen', published on 21 September 1914:

> They went with songs into battle, they were young,
> Straight of limb, true of eye, steady and aglow.
> They were staunch to the end against odds uncounted:
> They fell with their faces to the foe.

Requisitioning horses in East Dereham market-place, 1914. During the first week of the war, officers searched the countryside in motor cars looking for horses suitable for war service. Under the Defence of the Realm Act 1914 they were empowered to requisition these horses and wagons for military purposes. Some horses were returned, in cases of hardship caused by the loss of a working animal; however, nationally, 165,000 horses were drafted into service.

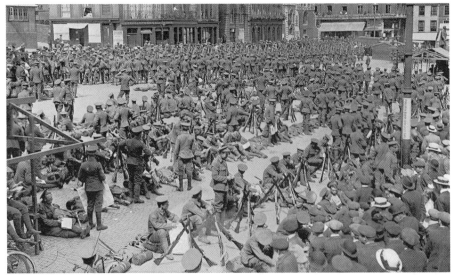

On 10 August 1914 over three thousand troops descended on Norwich market-place. Men of The Essex Regiment, previously stationed on the coast, had been withdrawn to the city. To the far right of the picture is the statue of the Duke of Wellington (now removed to Cathedral Close). Beneath him, standing 'morosely within a ring of bayonets' before an intrigued crowd, were four German 'spies'. In fact they were German waiters, captured from the Hotel de Paris at Cromer!

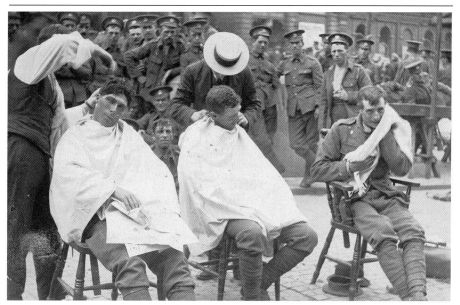

Local barbers brought chairs into Norwich market-place and gave the men of The Essex Regiment shaves and military haircuts.

Kitchener volunteers march up Guildhall Hill, Norwich, 1914. With patriotic fervour, the new armies were rapidly trained, and the Norfolk men were destined for the 12th and 18th (Eastern) Division proceeding to France and Flanders.

Kitchener volunteers on parade at Carrow, 1914. They were some of the 100,000 men required for the new armies who had responded to the poster showing Lord Kitchener with his imposing face and pointing finger, with the bold statement: 'Your King and Country Need YOU!' Because of the massive influx of volunteers, the issue of uniforms became piecemeal – a hat for one man, a tunic for another, so that for much of their early training they were in civvies. They were popularized at the time in a song:

> We are Fred Karno's Army
> The Rag-Time infantry.
> We cannot fight, we cannot shoot
> What God damn use are we?
> But when we get to Berlin,
> the Kaiser he will say –
> Hoch! Hoch! Mein Gott, what a bloody fine lot
> Fred Karno's sent today.

Great Eastern Railway clerical staff, who served with the 34th Division Signal Company, Royal Engineers (Norfolk Battalion). Under the schemes of Kitchener and Lord Ryder, local industries were encouraged to supply large numbers of men for the army. Friends, workmates and family members therefore had the chance to go to war together, in what became known as 'Pals' Battalions'.

Troops on Prince of Wales Road, Norwich, September 1914. By this time the great mobilization and troop movements were in full swing. Thousands of soldiers were moving to war stations and anti-invasion positions along the coast as well as to collation points for active service abroad. Horse lines and tent camps seemed to spring up on all available land, be it fine grazed park or fields. It was soon quite common to see troop transport columns jamming up Norfolk highways and byways.

Working together, men of the No. 15 Detachment, City of Norwich, British Red Cross Society, and Royal Army Medical Corps struggle to lay down a casualty from the first Battle of Ypres at Thorpe station, 17 October 1914. Wounded soldiers started arriving in Norfolk in seemingly endless train loads. Often crowds came to greet the boys home, even throwing flowers into the backs of ambulances leaving the station.

Men of the British Red Cross (Norwich Transport Company) unload ambulances at Thorpe Hospital, 1914. During the course of the war they dealt with 41,000 wounded in 322 convoys.

'There was rum, rum for the General's tum, in the stores, in the stores. . . .' I don't know about rum but there certainly seems to be plenty of Johnnie Walker Scotch whisky, sides of beef and bread. This is the 4th (Service) Battalion Essex Regiment stores, adjacent to the Goat Inn on Church Street, Wymondham.

Church parade for a detachment of the Royal Army Medical Corps, in Aylsham market-place, 1914.

The first parade of the Norwich VTC, 15 December 1914. With the fear of invasion, many men too old or unsuitable for military service still wanted to do their bit for the war effort. Following a great meeting in the Assembly Rooms of the Agricultural Hall, Norwich, 276 names were handed in, with the single aim of starting a Volunteer Training Corps – First World War equivalent of the Home Guard!

Invasion scares became rife towards the end of 1914. Under the Home Defence Scheme the observation and patrol defences of the British coast were entrusted to certain mounted and cycle corps of the Territorial Army. This task was entrusted to 1/6th (Territorial) Cyclist Battalion, The Norfolk Regiment, under the command of Col. Bernard Leathes Prior DSO, TD. It had headquarters at Park Hall, North Walsham, and detachments at Great Yarmouth, King's Lynn, Thetford, Fakenham, Ditchingham and Watton. The duty area stretched from Wells-on-Sea to Gorleston, and through the perishing winter of 1914 the men watched for any invasion threat.

The first bomb ever dropped in anger on a civilian target from an aircraft fell on Whitehall Yard, Wymondham Street, Sheringham, at about 8.30 p.m. on Tuesday 19 January 1915. This attack was devised by Adm. von Pohl, Chief of Imperial German Naval Staff, and the Kaiser himself. The attack was to be led by Fregattenkapitän Peter Strasser, Chief of the German Naval Airship Division. Three airships, the L3, L4 and L6 (under Strasser) from Nordholz, took off for the mission. However, the L6 developed engine trouble and had to turn back, much to the disgust of Strasser. The L4 made landfall over Bacton, her commander, Kapitänleutnant Magnus Count von Platen Hallermand, believed he was over the Humber and dropped a couple of bombs on Sheringham.

The first Zeppelin raid on Great Yarmouth, 19 January 1915. The L3, making landfall a short distance from the L4, proceeded to Great Yarmouth. Several people were hurt, and in the Drakes Buildings/St Peters Plain area Mrs Martha Taylor and Samuel Smith the shoemaker were killed. As the 'aerial baby-killer' left the town the detachment of the 6th (Cyclist) Battalion, The Norfolk Regiment, opened fire, causing superficial damage to the Zeppelin.

The first Zeppelin raid on King's Lynn, 19 January 1915. Swinging away from Sheringham, the L4 passed over Weybourne and Holt, and dropped a bomb over Snettisham, blast damaging the church windows. It then proceeded to King's Lynn, where it deposited high explosive and incendiary bombs, wrecking several houses and blowing large holes in the roads. Percy Goate and Mrs Maude Gazeley were both killed in Bentinck Street.

In January 1915 the Glamorgan Imperial Yeomanry (including many boys from Bridgend) arrived in Aylsham. The photograph is entitled 'All that was left of them', and a lone bugler with bandaged head sounds the battle call as the superimposed cannon shells fall around. Armed with rifles and fixed bayonets the men take aim as the lethal wheelbarrow and drainpipe artillery is wheeled into place.

Stationed at Holt Park Camp is the Montgomeryshire Imperial Yeomanry, complete with horse lines. Although horses were originally regarded as a viable mode of transport during the First World War, in active service almost all of the British yeomanry was dismounted.

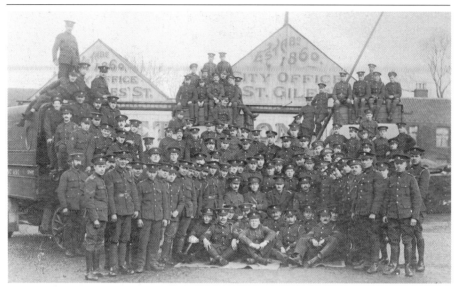

The headquarters staff of 977 Company, Army Service Corps Motor Transport, pile on to their lorries in St Giles Street, Norwich, March 1915. In addition to their own duties of military-vehicle maintenance, War Office transport duties and driving the war hospital's own ambulances, they worked closely with the Norfolk and Norwich Voluntary Transport Companies.

The Thorpe Annexe canteen and convalescent room of the Norfolk War Hospital, c. 1915. The canteen sold everything from McVitie & Price biscuits and Wills Woodbine cigarettes to fresh fruit and sweetheart badges. Thousands of letters and postcards were sent home from here and were often written to the accompanying sound of a pianist, who had been blinded by gas at Ypres.

Red Cross nurses of the Thorpe War Hospital. Nursing volunteers had rapidly assembled uniforms, even having to make and sew the red cross on their apron.

Tent wards, Thorpe War Hospital, 1915. With British casualties totalling over a million, every bed was desperately needed. All available floor space became occupied and eventually drastic measures had to be taken. The wounded were housed temporarily in tent wards in the grounds of the hospital.

'It's a long, long way to Tipperary, but my heart's right there', and I am sure it was with the gypsy dancer, ventriloquist, singers and comedy dance trio of HMS *Nelson*, the Tipperary Concert Party. It brought a little ray of sunshine to the wounded in the hospitals and tent wards of the Norwich war hospitals.

Hoveton Hall VAD Hospital, 1915. With the hospitals and their grounds filling up, eventually any suitable building was used to house the wounded. Sixty-two Auxiliary or Voluntary Aid Detachment hospitals were set up in Norfolk. Operated by members of both the British Red Cross Society and the Order of St John of Jerusalem, they treated over 35,736 patients between 1914 and 1919.

Walsingham VAD Hospital, 1915. Sitting on the wall are three patients in the familiar garb of wounded soldiers of the First World War. When convalescing they were issued with a pale blue jacket, grey trousers, white shirt and scarlet tie and, as seen here, they were allowed to retain their hat, or bonnet in the case of the Scots, to denote their regiment.

'Happy as the day when the sergeant gets his pay.' These lucky fellows are 'C' Squadron, the East Riding of Yorkshire Imperial Yeomanry (Lancers), on pay parade at Riddlesworth. Wages ranged from 1s 2d for cavalrymen to 5s 4d for Troop Sergeants, with a messing and clothing allowance of 3d a day.

This fine study shows a machine-gunner and his number two of the Lincolnshire Yeomanry manning a Maxim 08 machine-gun on Garboldisham Rifle Range. This weapon was used by both the British and German Armies throughout the war. It was capable of firing a steady five hundred rounds a minute, fed through on long canvas belts. A heavy weapon, it weighed 76–80 lb, and was water-cooled by a jacket sleeving, the barrel holding 7 quarts of water.

Harry Daniels was born on 13 December 1882. He was the thirteenth child of a trading couple, who built their business around a small bakery-cum-confectionery shop in Wymondham. Sadly, his parents died young, and the five youngest children, including Harry, were consigned to the orphanage. At eighteen he enlisted in the Rifle Brigade. After serving twelve years as a professional soldier, and having attained the rank of Company Sergeant Major, he was to face the ultimate test. On 12 March 1915 at Neuve Chapelle it was the third day of an ill-fated offensive. 'A' and 'B' Companies of the 2nd Battalion Rifle Brigade had been virtually annihilated. Just before 5.00 p.m. 'C' and 'D' received the order to 'Attack in fifteen minutes'. Facing severe machine-gun fire and a mass of uncut barbed wire 15 yards from the trench, it was suicide. CSM Daniels cried 'Get some nippers!' and he and Pte. Tom Noble proceeded into No Man's Land to cut the wire, thereby saving many lives in the attack. Sadly Tom Noble, also awarded the VC, was killed but CSM Harry Daniels returned to Norwich as its first VC hero.

Men of the 1/2 Norfolk Royal Field Artillery Battery, 26 May 1915. Back row, left to right: A/Bdr. E. Spalding, A/Bdr. F. Allen, Bdr. W. Gibbons, Bdr. H.J. Fousham, Bdr. E. Foulsham, Bdr. E. Cannell, Bdr. H.J. Heyhoe, U/A Bdr. A.C. Rogers, U/A Bdr. A. Hook, U/A Bdr. T. Goodall, A/Bdr. S. Wilson, A/Bdr. G. Bloomfield, A/Bdr. F. Sexton. Third row: Cpl. H. Garrard, A/Bdr. R.C. Moore, Bdr. H.C. Maybury, Bdr. V.R. Simmet, Cpl. Sdlr. A.E. Pull, Cpl. G. Bull, Cpl. W. Macartney, Cpl. S. Tallant, Cpl. W. Chapman, Cpl. Fitter C. Flowers, Cpl. SS E.R. Willie, Bdr. A. Holman, U/A Bdr. P. Sparrow, Bdr. W. Melton. Second row: BQMS M. Nunn, 2nd Lt. A.F. Culham, Lt. M.A. Castle, Capt. O. Miles, Maj. Chas E. Hodges, Lt. W.R. Kempson, 2nd Lt. F.E. Danvers, BSM J.A. Lawson, Sgt. E.A. Kewley. Seated on the ground: Sgt. E. Neal, Sgt. E.M. Glasheen, Farr. Sgt. W.H. Hart, Sgt. Curtis-Wilson, Fitter Sgt. G.R. Fowler, Sgt. D. Vout.

By July 1915 the East Riding of Yorkshire Imperial Yeomanry had moved from Riddlesworth to Costessey Hall. The men are seen here awaiting Sunday dinner and it looks as if they will be tucking into stewed beef and vegetables, a stark contrast to the fare they were to have just two months later in the putrid atmosphere of the Dardanelles – that is if the rations even got through.

The 6th (Cyclist) Battalion, The Royal Sussex Regiment, arrived in Norfolk in August 1915. It was based in Stalham, in the field opposite Mill House on the old Yarmouth Road, and was housed in tented billets.

The aftermath of the Zeppelin raid on East Dereham on 9 September 1915. The town received extensive damage. James Taylor, general dealer, Harry Patterson, watchmaker and jeweller, and L/Cpl. Alfred Pomeroy of the 2/1st City of London Yeomanry were killed and several were injured, including two who died of their wounds. Seen here is the wreckage of Church Street, where the body of L/Cpl. Pomeroy was found.

The band of His Majesty's Royal Marines on top of a Norwich Electric Tramways Company tram in Orford Place. This was just one of the events held as part of a massive recruiting drive for all arms of the Royal Navy, Royal Marines and Royal Naval Division. The call was for men between the ages of eighteen and thirty-eight to volunteer, and was given out by Lt. Spry RNVR and Cdr. the Hon. Rupert Guiness MP at a meeting in the Corn Hall on Saturday 17 July 1915.

A Sopwith seaplane at the Royal Naval Air Service's North Sea Air Station, South Denes, Great Yarmouth. At the outbreak of war the main functions of sorties flown from here were coastal defence, patrolling the North Sea for Zeppelins and monitoring enemy shipping. The final active sortie of the war flown from the station was on 5 August 1918, when Maj. Egbert Cadbury shot down Zeppelin L70.

The funeral procession of Lt. Hillyard, Royal Naval Air Service, leaving St Peter's Church, Great Yarmouth. He was killed engaging a Zeppelin raider at Bacton-on-Sea on 11 September 1915.

The 1st (City of Norwich) Battalion, Norfolk Volunteers, being inspected by Col. the Earl of Leicester GCVO, CM, ADC, Regimental Commandant, accompanied by Lt.-Col. Leathes Prior VD, 26 September 1915. Although the average age of the volunteers was forty-four they were well trained and undertook many varied duties, ranging from armed guards on bridges, utilities and transport centres against enemy sabotage to guiding British airships into hangars. They were cruelly called 'the Cripples Brigade' or 'England's last hope!'

1st Norwich (CLB) Battalion, King's Royal Rifle Corps Cadets, *c.* 1915. These lads worked with the City of Norwich Volunteers in the capacity of observers and messenger runners. They also paraded on many occasions with their fine band and had the honour of providing a guard for duty when Queen Alexandra visited Norwich on 12 October 1918.

An artist's impression of the execution of Nurse Edith Cavell. Born in 1865, she was the daughter of the Vicar of Swardeston, and her life was dedicated to caring for others. Working from her clinic in Brussels she treated both German and British troops. She became part of an underground escape network for Allied soldiers, but was betrayed by George Carten Quien and condemned under charge of 'conducting soldiers to the enemy'. She was executed on 12 October 1915.

'Another Hundred Recruits', all joining the 2nd East Anglian Field Ambulance, Royal Army Medical Corps. The Territorial Force poses in front of its headquarters on Bethel Street, Norwich, 1915. They were probably some of the last true volunteers from Norfolk as conscription of men for military service became necessary in the winter of 1915. On 24 January 1916 the first Compulsory Service Act was passed and implemented on 2 March 1916.

A detachment of the Royal Naval Anti-Aircraft Mobile Brigade at North Walsham, April 1916. The detachment was sent armed with Rolls-Royce armoured cars and Royal Enfield motorbikes to operate defences on the Norfolk coast against the constant threat of Zeppelin air raids. It demanded that the Happisburgh lightship turn its light out as it was considered that the Zeppelins used it as a beacon to guide them in. There was, however, an early warning system established in the form of coops of pheasants at Winterton dunes, as it was discovered the birds became restless when aero-engines approached.

The officers of the recruiting staff of the 9th Rural District recruiting area, for the county of Norfolk, 1917. Back row, left to right: Lt. C.A.B. Hadley, RO, King's Lynn; Capt. H.W.M. Wilkin, King's Lynn; Lt. A. Oldman, RO, Wroxham; Lt. J.H. Farmer, HQ Norwich; Capt. S.R.C. Willoughby, RO, Attleborough; Capt. H.D. Bennett, RO, Norwich. Front row: Capt. H.A. Williams, Munitions Area RO, HQ Norwich; Lt. F.G. Harris, HQ Norwich; Capt. J.C. Blofield, Wroxham Sub-Area; Maj. E.M. Hansell, Cromer Sub-Area; Maj. H.C. Corlette, Chief Recruiting Officer; Capt. H.S. Sutherland, Area Registration Officer, HQ Norwich; Maj. J.H. Kennedy, Attleborough; Lt. E.F. Routh-Clarke, Commander, Norwich Sub-Area.

Captured German field guns put on display in front of Norwich Castle are inspected by the Mayor of Norwich, Sir George Chamberlin DL.

Female war workers at Pulham airship station, *c.* 1916. Each woman holds an item representing the type of work she was doing.

Norwich Munition Girls dressed in their 'National Shell' overalls. These girls worked night and day to feed the guns for the 1916 summer offensive. If they did not carefully tuck in all their hair it could be turned ginger by the cordite used. If exposure to it was not checked it could prove fatal!

Miss Burton Fanning enrols and presents arm bands to Land Army Girls at Mr J. Thistleton Smith's farm, West Barsham, 1917.

Great Yarmouth welcomes America, 4 July 1918. Over five hundred American troops arrived at Vauxhall station, from where they marched down North Quay to the official reception in front of the Town Hall. Afterwards a baseball match was played at the Wellesley Recreation Ground, and the day was completed with a dance at the Assembly Rooms.

NORFOLK CONSTABULARY
NOTICE!
SHOOTING HOMING PIGEONS

Killing, Wounding or Molesting Carrier or Homing Pigeons

is punishable under the Defence of the Realm Regulations by

SIX MONTHS' IMPRISONMENT OR £100 FINE.

The public are reminded that Carrier and Homing Pigeons are doing valuable work for the Government, and are requested to assist in the suppression of the shooting of these birds.

A REWARD of £5

will be paid by the General Officer Commanding Northern Army, Home Defence, for information securing conviction for killing or concealing Naval or Military Carrier Pigeons.

Information should be given to the Police or nearest Military Post or to the General Officer Commanding Northern Army, H. D., Norwich.

Any person who finds a Carrier or Homing Pigeon dead or incapable of flight and who neglects forthwith to hand it over or send it to some military post or police constable in the neighbourhood with information as to the place where the pigeon was found; or, having obtained information as to any Carrier or Homing Pigeon being killed or found incapable for flight, neglects forthwith to communicate the information to a military post or to a police constable in the neighbourhood is liable, on conviction, to the punishment above described.

J. H. MANDER, *Captain,*

County Police Station,   **Chief Constable.**
Castle Meadow, Norwich,

November 1917.

Roberts & Co., Printers, Ten Bell Lane, Norwich.

A poster warning of the consequences of tampering with vital lines of communication.

Norwich Special Constables on parade at Chapel Field Gardens, August 1917. Behind the front row are volunteers, recently sworn in at the Guildhall before the City Magistrates. They were also issued with their first uniform, an arm band with a badge, a whistle and a truncheon.

The mighty Mark IV tank manoeuvres in front of Norwich Guildhall for Tank Week (Monday 1 to Saturday 6 April 1918). The tank had arrived by train from the secret tank training area on Lord Iveagh's estate at Elvedon. Tank Week raised £1,957,000 for the War Loan.

Great Yarmouth Tank Week, 1918. Although unable to obtain a real tank the town was not to be outdone. Large hoardings were painted and fixed to a tram, and the model was even given a number from the fishing-boat series – YH777.

Norwich market-place at the eleventh hour of the eleventh day of the eleventh month, 1918. The officers and men of a battalion from The Bedfordshire Regiment fix bayonets and hold their hats aloft in one almighty cheer: the First World War is over!

Harry Cator MM, CdeG, was born on 24 January 1894. A modest man, he was the son of a railway worker from Drayton, and was the most decorated Norfolk soldier of either war. On 9 April 1917 his battalion, the 7th East Surreys, went over the top near Arras, France. As the situation became desperate he advanced across No Man's Land, picking up a Lewis gun and ammunition. He reached the enemy trench, knocked out its defences and held it, enabling the capture of one hundred prisoners and five machine-guns. For this courageous action he was awarded the Victoria Cross.

Sidney James Day was born in Norwich on 3 July 1891 and was educated at St Mark's School, Lakenham. He was awarded the VC while serving as a corporal with the 11th Battalion, The Suffolk Regiment, in the line at Priel Wood, Malakoff Farm, east of Hargicourt, France. The incident occurred on 26 August 1917. Day's section had cleared numerous enemy trenches and upon his return a stick bomb fell into a nearby trench. Day seized it and hurled it back! After clearing this trench he remained at his post for sixty-six hours.

Gordon Muriel Flowerdew was born at Billingford Hall, in the Waveney valley, on 2 January 1885. On 30 March 1918, while in command of a squadron of Lord Strathcona's Horse (a Canadian mounted regiment), he led a charge against a heavily entrenched enemy position north-east of Bois de Morevil. Charging again they broke the line, but not without receiving heavy casualties, including Lt. Flowerdew. He died on Easter Day, and his Victoria Cross was promulgated a month later.

Arthur Henry Cross MM was born on 13 December 1884, the son of a Shipham wheelwright. He was awarded the Victoria Cross while serving with the 40th Battalion, machine-gun Corps. On 25 March 1918 at Ervillers, France, he crossed to the enemy trenches with his revolver and forced several Germans to surrender and to carry their guns with tripods to Allied lines. Handing over the prisoners, he then collected teams for his guns and repelled a very heavy attack by the enemy.

SECTION THREE

Aftermath and the Inter-war Years

Tasburgh British Legion church parade, 1926.

Two 'H' class British submarines lie alongside their war trophy, a captured German coastal type submarine at Hall Quay, Great Yarmouth, 1919. This UB boat was capable of 8 knots on the surface and a maximum of 6 knots submerged. These vessels had been deployed with UC boats from their base at Flanders, and were often used for laying mines along the east coast of England.

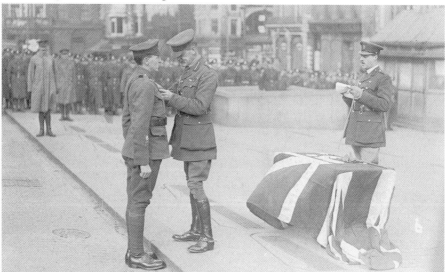

On 29 January 1919 Norwich market-place was lined with companies from each battalion of the 193rd Brigade, Military Police, and a military band. The occasion was the presentation of medals to some returned soldiers for gallantry in the field by Maj.-Gen. Sir J.E. Capper KCB, while each citation was read by Col. Hare.

Returned servicemen from Worstead proudly wearing their medals awarded for service in the First World War. Often the effects of the war were felt most profoundly in these rural villages. Sixty years later one veteran wrote: 'There can never be another war like the Great War, nor the comradeship and endurance we knew then. I think, perhaps, men are not like that now.'

Following Armistice Day, the feeling across the country was that peace should be officially celebrated with those who had returned from the conflict. Seen here is North Walsham's Peace Day, held on Saturday 19 June 1919.

The memorial to Edith Cavell, patriot and martyr, was unveiled on 12 October 1918 in its original position in front of The Maids' Head Hotel. After the war Nurse Cavell's body was returned to the county she loved and was buried in Lifes' Green near Norwich Cathedral, where memorial services are still held for her on the Sunday nearest to the anniversary of her execution.

Two boys from Watts' Naval Training School pause after sounding the Last Post at the opening of Swanton Morley War Memorial. This was erected in memory of the eleven men from the parish who died in the First World War. Memorials like this are found all across Norfolk, a poignant reminder of the horrific loss of life and its devastating impact on rural communities.

Norwich collectors for the first Earl Haig Fund Poppy Day. Organized by the Norfolk County War Pensioners Committee and British Legion, the first Poppy Day was held on 11 November 1921. Disabled ex-servicemen worked all year making the poppies which, in 1921, helped to raise £106,000 for the benefit of widows, orphans and the estimated 500,000 disabled British ex-servicemen.

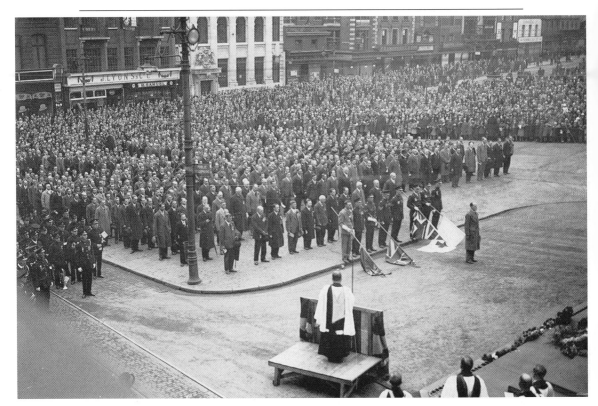

A massive parade of First World War veterans fills Norwich market-place on Armistice Day, 1920. Over 100,000 Norfolk men fought in the war, and one in nine was killed; in fact 2½ per cent of the entire population of this county never returned. Everybody lost someone they knew or cared for. Tens of thousands were wounded, handicapped or mentally unbalanced. Those who remained at home could never really understand what happened in 'the war to end all wars'.

The R33 over the hangars at the airship station, Pulham St Mary, 1925. Once a familiar sight the 'Pulham Pigs' flew from 1915 till the early 1930s, when Britain abandoned its airship programme because of numerous costly accidents. The R33, one of two giant Zeppelins surrendered to Britain after the war, was no exception. On 16 April 1925 the R33 broke from its moorings with twenty-three officers and men on board. As they fought to regain control she drifted over the North Sea. Twenty-eight hours later they finally succeeded in regaining control and the R33 returned to home base, though the nose of the airship was badly smashed. The image was featured widely in the national press.

'Guns aloft!' Boys from Watts' Naval Training School take part in a Winchester rifle and fitness drill display at the annual Open Day, 31 July 1925. Purchased in June 1901, the building at North Elmham was equipped, complete with necessary staff, by Sir Fenwick Shadforth Watts and presented to Dr Barnardo as a school for three hundred boys.

Men of the Royal Norfolk Veterans Association parade for Edward, Prince of Wales, at the Royal Norfolk Show during the 1920s. The total length of service with the colours of all the members of the association at the time was over a thousand years.

Territorials of the 5th Battalion, the Norfolk Regiment, marching in short-sleeve order near Weybourne. Columns of such soldiers on training camps all along the Norfolk coast in the summer months were a familiar sight throughout the 1930s.

Weybourne Camp, on the clifftop and Muckleborough Hill, was briefly home for thousands of soldiers over the years. They would come here for a few weeks' training or for weekend camps, which were held all year round. Many a night was spent enduring the worst of the weather as it rolled straight in from the cold North Sea.

King George VI, accompanied by Capt. R.F. Humphrey, inspects a guard of honour drawn from all companies of the 4th (Territorial) Battalion, The Royal Norfolk Regiment, at the opening of the new City Hall on 29 October 1938.

SECTION FOUR

The Second World War

Members of North Walsham St John Ambulance Brigade on exercise wearing gas masks, June 1940.

TO MY PEOPLE.

At this grave moment in the struggle between my people and a highly organised enemy who has transgressed the Laws of Nations and changed the ordinance that binds civilized Europe together, I appeal to you.

I rejoice in my Empire's effort, and I feel pride in the voluntary response from my Subjects all over the world who have sacrificed home, fortune, and life itself, in order that another may not inherit the free Empire which their ancestors and mine have built.

I ask you to make good these sacrifices.

The end is not in sight. More men and yet more are wanted to keep my Armies in the Field, and through them to secure Victory and enduring Peace.

In ancient days the darkest moment has ever produced in men of our race the sternest resolve.

I ask you, men of all classes, to come forward voluntarily and take your share in the fight.

In freely responding to my appeal, you will be giving your support to our brothers, who, for long months, have nobly upheld Britain's past traditions, and the glory of her Arms.

George R.J.

A personal message from King George VI was pasted up on post office walls and council notice-boards, after the distribution of posters announcing the proclamation of war on 3 September 1939.

Digging air-raid shelters in Chapel Field Gardens, Norwich, February 1939. The Nazi aggression put Europe into turmoil, and trenches had already been dug as some means of shelter from the new Blitzkrieg.

ARP wardens of Group I, Division I, Post H8, based at the children's home in Turners Road, Norwich, 1940. Drawn from residents in the St Benedicts/Dereham Road area, many faces will be remembered, especially (standing, far right) the late Frank Kirby of the cycle shop at 5 St Benedicts. Trained since the late '30s in all aspects of air-raid precautions, from stirrup pumps to gas masks, the wardens will always be remembered for their strict observation of the blackout and for the call 'Put that light out!'.

EXPANSION OF THE
TERRITORIAL ARMY

TO MEN OF NORFOLK

Owing to wanton aggression and attempts at world domination by certain powers the peace of the whole world and the most sacred traditions of all the democracies are threatened. Therefore, we as a nation must be ready to meet and answer any such aggression.

The Government has decided that an immediate expansion of the Territorial Army shall be carried out. This means that all Field Force Units of the Territorial Army in the County of Norfolk, after being brought up to their full establishment, will have to be doubled again in numbers.

We must be prepared. REMEMBER ENGLAND EXPECTS EVERY MAN TO DO HIS DUTY and that the personal sacrifice called for is a small price to pay as an insurance for world peace and for the safety of all we hold dear in this life.

We MUST now prove to the world that our VOLUNTARY SYSTEM of which we are justly proud is a reality, not a mere phrase, by the manhood of the nation coming forward and giving their services in the armed forces of the nation.

The Whole World Awaits Your Answer

We earnestly appeal to you, Men of Norfolk, to join one of the undermentioned Territorial Army Units.

Please apply AT ONCE either personally or by letter or telephone to any of the following addresses

UNIT	ADDRESS	Tel. No.	UNIT	ADDRESS	Tel. No.
219th Anti-Tank Battery Headquarters and	Drill Hall, Cattle Market, Norwich		H.Q. Company	Drill Hall, Wellesley Street King's Lynn	
220th Anti-Tank Battery	" " Spinners Lane, Swaffham		" B " Company	" " Next to the Church Lane Fakenham	
4th Bn. The Royal Norfolk Regt. Bn. H.Q. and "A" Coy.	" " Chapel Field Rd., Norwich		" C " Company	" " Pound Lane, Aylsham	
" B " Company	" " Queens Rd. Attleborough		" D " Company	" " Gersingham	
" C " Company	" " Harleston		250th. Field Company R. E.	" " Cattle Market, Norwich	
" D " Company	" " Drill Hall, York Road Great Yarmouth		163rd. (E. A.) Field Ambulance	" " No. 2, Hiliary Avenue, Plumstead Rd. Norwich	
5th Bn. The Royal Norfolk Regt. Bn. H.Q. and H.Q. Coy.	" " Norwich Rd., E. Dereham		41st. A.A. Divisional R.A.O.C. Workshop Company	22, Tombland, Norwich	

GOD SAVE THE KING

A. E. SOMAN & CO., LTD., ST. ANDREW'S PRINTING WORKS, NORWICH.

A recruitment poster, 1939. After the reduction of the Territorial Army in the inter-war years a large and rapid expansion was required to bring it up to fighting strength.

Officers and men of 'B' Company, 4th Battalion, The Royal Norfolk Regiment (TA), Attleborough, 1939. When up to strength, three territorial battalions of The Royal Norfolks were furnished for war service. As part of the British 18th Division they ended up as prisoners of war after the fall of Singapore. Seventy per cent never returned; they were killed or died of horrific disease while in Japanese hands.

Motor Transport Platoon, 70th (Young Soldiers) Battalion, The Royal Norfolk Regiment, 1940. The battalion was under Army orders of 19 September 1940 and comprised young soldiers who had volunteered before they were officially due to be called up. They were formed into 70th Battalions throughout the line infantry. This battalion was based in The Crescent, Chapel Field Gardens. Under the command of Lt.-Col. E. Thistleton-Smith and the watchful eye of R.S.M. Swingler they trained all across the county for six weeks and then were placed in defensive positions throughout the Battle of Britain.

Militia recruits messing 11 o'clock tea at Britannia Barracks. Misleadingly titled, they were in fact the first conscripted servicemen of the Second World War. Nationally there was only one intake of 35,000 men recruited under the 1939 Military Training Act. On reaching the age of twenty they were to undergo six months' military training in one of the three services, followed by three and a half years in the Reserve, during which time they 'might be recalled in an emergency for full time duty'. Consequently they were destined to serve a good deal longer than six months.

'Fitness to do the job' was the priority, as ably demonstrated here by men of the Training Battalion, The Royal Norfolk Regiment, in autumn 1939. The training was rapid and intensive under the 'vicious' and demanding eyes of the physical training instructor sergeants.

A Royal Norfolk Regiment recruit company skill-at-arms lecture, autumn 1939. The instructor sergeant: 'This is the No. 1, Mk III Lee-Enfield breechloading magazine rifle of the bolt type. Weight about 8 lb 14 oz, effective range 600 yd. It fires .303 in ammunition, magazine holds 10 rounds – you will be expected to achieve 15 rounds per minute rapid fire!'

Evacuees to North Walsham, 1939. On 1 September 1939 war seemed imminent and the first evacuation took place of 827,000 schoolchildren, 524,000 mothers and children under school age, nearly 13,000 expectant mothers, 7,000 blind, crippled or otherwise handicapped people and 103,000 teachers and helpers from urban areas such as London and its boroughs. These evacuees are from Edmonton and Bethnal Green. After friction started between the children, the school day was divided; the local children attended from 9.00 a.m. to 12.30 p.m. and the evacuees from 1.30 p.m. to 5.00 p.m. One lady had a terrible shock after housing two evacuees; she went to their bedroom and found the wallpaper torn off in strips. They had been looking for bugs, imagining that 'The fifth column is everywhere!'.

Police Headquarters, Thorpe Road, Norwich, September 1939. This was just one of the many public buildings to be protected with walls of sandbags, and it was soon to have all the windows taped over to prevent flying glass caused by bomb blasts.

The first crews of the Norfolk County Council Casualty Services, 1939. Several such mobile units sprung up across the county and were operated by members of the St John Ambulance and the British Red Cross Society. Their function was to help recover the thousands of casualties anticipated as a result of the possible blitz on our cities. As well as medical supplies each station held a stock of hundreds of compressed cardboard coffins.

The burial of a German airman, Sheringham, 1939. At 3.00 a.m. on Wednesday 5 December 1939 a twin-engined Heinkel III crashed on Sheringham beach. The bodies of the two crew members were washed ashore soon afterwards. At this time it was still regarded as the 'phoney' or 'gentlemen's' war and this is typified by the treatment of the dead airman. The observer Oberfeldwebel Emil Rodel was buried at Bircham Newton with full military honours. Oberleutnant zur See W. Wodtke was taken to Sheringham Town Cemetery in a coffin draped with a swastika flag. The Last Post was sounded and an eleven-gun salute fired. A member of the town's British Legion even dropped a Flanders poppy on to the coffin.

The Steward & Patterson's Brewery firemen with one of their Coventry Victor trailer pumps. This was one of about a hundred operating from Auxiliary Fire Service stations within the Norwich area.

Men of Steward & Patterson Auxiliary Fire Service Patrol No. 21 in front of their fire station at the Pockthorpe Brewery, Barrack Street. They are standing on their converted lorry, which is loaded with rescue equipment, hose, foam branch, rope and extension ladder. The vehicle itself towed a trailer pump.

Cromer lifeboatmen in front of No. 1 boathouse at the end of the pier, *c.* 1941. As if the lifeboatmen's job were not hard enough in peacetime, during the war they had to proceed unarmed into 'active waters', where there were added dangers of E-boats, mines and random attacks from enemy aircraft. They were needed more than ever to assist shipping damaged in action, and sometimes spent many hours searching for ditched aircrew. Pictured on the far right of the group is their legendary cox'n Henry Blogg.

Men of the Sheringham lifeboat bring ashore crew members from the *Boston Trader*. The ship was about 3 miles off Cley at 12.15 p.m. on 9 February 1940 when she was bombed and caught fire. By 12.33 p.m. the Sheringham lifeboat was launched across sand at low tide. The ship's crew, now in a small boat which barely showed above the waterline, was rescued at 1.30 p.m.

Pilots of 242 Squadron at RAF Coltishall, 1940. The squadron, which consisted largely of Canadian personnel, was one of the last units to fight in France before the country fell. Its surviving members returned to Coltishall on 20 June 1940. Under their new commanding officer, Sqn. Ldr. Douglas Bader, they returned to operational status and served with distinction. During the Battle of Britain they flew Hurricanes as part of 12 Group alongside the Spitfires of 66 Squadron. From left to right: P/Os D. Crowley-Milling, H.N. Tamblyn and P.S. Turner, Sgt. J.E. Saville (on the wing). P/Os N.N. Campbell and W.L. McKnight, Sqn. Ldr. D. Bader, Flt. Lt. G.E. Ball, P/Os M.C. Homer and M.K. Brown.

Men of 325th Coastal Battery, 514th Coast Regiment (Anti-Aircraft), 2nd Corps, based at Great Yarmouth. Seen here during gun drill, they are responding to the warning of 'Enemy raiders approaching'; camouflage nets are folded back as the gunners race to their positions.

The guns of Weybourne Anti-Aircraft Battery blaze. In peacetime, when it was an artillery practice camp, the flash of the guns at night was a familiar sight. Now the guns were fired for real, as Britain's first line of land defence against the Luftwaffe.

A Dornier 17 on display at Eaton Park, Norwich, September 1940. The plane, under the command of Joachim Hellmers, was caught by anti-aircraft fire while intent on raiding factories in Coventry. It crash-landed in a field just outside Norwich and attempts by the crew to destroy the plane failed. It was captured complete, towed through the city and put on show.

16 Group, Royal Observer Corps, Mundesley Post, *c.* 1941. Possibly one of the loneliest vocations during the war was that of the observer. For hours one would simply watch and listen, often on the coast in foul weather. Dr Lund, pictured here, is well prepared. Strategically positioned posts with radio links provided the control centre on Lime Tree Road, Norwich, with vital information on enemy aircraft, and no doubt saved thousands of lives.

'A' Company, 5th Battalion, Norfolk Home Guard, from North Walsham, *c.* 1943. Back row, left to right; Dan Webster; -?-, -?- 'Muggy' MacLean, -?-, Les Willer, ? Wiseman. Third row: Harry Davison, ? Howlett, ? Lawrence, Stanley Davison, Ralph Pardon, George Barratt, Stanley Plummer, Jack Pinner. Second row: Charlie Strait, Ernie Willey, -?-, -?-, Bob Mills, Ted Stratton, ? Mace, -?-, Claude Leatherdale. Front row: Sgt. Alf Rawlings, Sgt. Bob Davison, a visiting CSM, Capt. Chandler (Company Commander), Lt. 'Lawyer' Bell, Sgt. Alan Wright, Cpl. Jack Beckenham, Cpl. Amiss. They are pictured in front of the Paston Grammar School, which was the battalion HQ; the men trained in the gymnasium, school yard and on the school field. At stand down the battalion had 77 officers and 1,724 other ranks, and companies stretched as far apart as Mundesley and Scottow.

North Walsham Cable Repeater Station Home Guard, *c.* 1943. Officially they were members of 'B' Company, 6th (34 GPO) Battalion, Cambridgeshire Regiment, Home Guard. Back row, left to right: Jack Taylor, Mr Strapps (postmaster), Frank Mann, Charlie Larkins, George Oakley, Lenny Brown (inspector of engineers), 'Tubby' Cutting, Jimmy Duncan, Edgar Richardson (postman). Middle row: Cpl. Bob Lancaster, Sgt. Bertie Manning (survey officer); Cpl. Edgar Cook (gang foreman). Front row: Cyril Chatten, Bertie Lawrence, Derek Manning. Directives were given for the GPO's own Home Guard to protect the local communications network from the Cambridge headquarters. Initially armed with pick-axes, these men worked a day at the station then, if it was their turn, they would return and do guard for the station from 7.00 p.m. to dawn. After the war it was found that most of the equipment had been removed from the station in 1939 and in effect all that while they had been guarding nothing.

Wroxham and Ormesby Broads flotilla, November 1940. These patrol boats watched the waters and skies above inland waterways for invaders or attempted landings by seaplanes. Originally pleasure-craft, these motorboats were requisitioned and fitted with Lewis guns. They operated under Cdr. B. Youatt, RN, as part of 2nd Corps, 213th Brigade, 18th (sdv) Division.

Winston Churchill, on his visit to the east coast defences, inspects men of the 2nd Cambridgeshire Regiment at Holt on 7 August 1940.

On 23 August 1940 King George VI visited Gorleston as part of his review of the east coast defences. He was received by a guard of honour of the 4th (Territorial) Battalion, The Royal Norfolk Regiment. He then inspected this parade of officers and men from minesweepers. As he left he was given three hearty cheers by all on parade.

Paratroopers prepare to blow open the doors of Norwich Castle. This was as part of a massive assault exercise codenamed Operation Bulldog, which took place over four days in the Eastern Command Area in June 1941.

ATS girls with a height finder at Weybourne Camp, October 1941. The girls were taught how to operate the 3.7 in anti-aircraft guns (in the background) but official regulations stated that women were not allowed to fire them apart from dummy practice rounds – a male soldier had to fire the live shell.

A crashed Junkers 88 on Weybourne beach, 3 May 1941. This bomber was part of the Luftwaffe unit 1/KG.30 based at Aalborg in Denmark and had set out the previous evening for a raid on Liverpool. Hit by anti-aircraft fire from near the Wash, the aircraft was forced to ditch in the sea 300 yards from Sparrow Gap. The crew, Erwin Gieger (pilot), Walter Seeberg, Helmut Laser and Richard Altmeyer, escaped with minor injuries and paddled in their emergency dinghy to the shore. There they were arrested and escorted to the Sheringham Hotel.

During the sunny spell of July 1941 the public was allowed access to the beaches, which had been sealed for so long. This sentry of the 2/5th West Yorks at Sheringham is keeping a watchful eye to see that visitors do not stray.

A bomb-disposal team in Gorleston. At 2.28 a.m. on 12 June 1941 Duke Road, Lowestoft Road and Frederick Road were hit by three HE bombs. Four people were killed and one was injured. The device in Frederick Road did not go off and the Royal Engineers bomb-disposal team was called there to de-activate it. Here, they stand relieved around the 4,000 pounder.

The NAAFI, situated on the site of Bunting's Store in Rampant Horse Street, which was badly damaged in the Norwich blitz of 1942. The Navy, Army and Air Force Institute established such entertainment centres across the country for troops. Many jibed at the Army-sponsored Entertainments National Services Association (ENSA) performers who appeared here, renaming it 'Every Night Something Awful'. One thing always appreciated was, however, the 2,000 meals and snacks a day, from rabbit pie and fish and chips to sponge pudding and Nelson cake.

Men of Lawrence & Scott's Works Fire Brigade, National Fire Service, No. 13 Fire Force 'A' Division, 1942. Their skill was undoubted; they won numerous shields and awards for their turnout, performance and accuracy with their light trailer pumps. They were not to know what horrors they were to face later that year.

St Lawrence's Church is silhouetted by the inferno in Norwich city during the night of 27/28 April 1942. Hitler had launched his Baedeker Blitz, aimed at the destruction of important historical cities of Great Britain in retaliation for RAF bombing raids on the ancient German city of Lübeck, and in an attempt to break morale.

Rampant Horse Street, the morning after the night raid of 29/30 April 1942. After the firefighters had spent hours tackling the blaze, taking thousands of gallons of water from the river and reservoirs, Norwich was still burning.

A crater at St Benedict's Gates, 30 April 1942. Some thought the end of the world had come! Here, men struggle with exposed mains in an attempt to start sorting out the mess. Rescue teams pull people and animals from the rubble and people patch up their homes if they can. Over 297 high-explosive bombs, weighing more than 95 tons, and thousands of incendiaries had been dropped on Norwich during two nights of bombing in April 1942. A total of 231 people were killed and 689 were wounded.

The king speaks to Civil Defence messenger boys. Among them is John Grix, aged fifteen. After continually running vital messages across the blitz-torn city, he was blown off his bicycle and blistered from the intense heat. He was awarded the British Empire Medal for his devotion to duty.

H.M. The King talks to Civil Defence Volunteers

H.R.H. The Duke of Kent at a bombed site

Centre
H.R.H. The Duke of Kent inspecting Civil Defence Services

H.M. The King at the Norfolk & N'ch Hospital

H.R.H. The Duke of Kent inspecting the Home, Guard

Views of the visit to Norwich by the Duke of Kent on Tuesday 26 May and the surprise visit of King George VI on Tuesday 13 October 1942. By seeing the damage for themselves and meeting many of the victims, they aimed to show the nation's concern for the cities which were suffering from the latest blitz campaign. Morale was certainly boosted as fine parades were held in the city centre in honour of the occasions.

The funeral of Sam Bussey, 1942. The sirens had wailed, hailing a blitz on a scale that no Norwich citizen could have imagined. The call went out for the firemen, who rushed from the Bethel Street station. Sam, who was in command of the fire engine, took the crew to the Westwick Street area, which had been blown apart, and attempts were being made to quell the fireball of the city station. With bombs falling all around Sam went to Oak Street to try to save some horses from a stable. Suddenly a bomb fell very close, wounding firemen Len Strivens and Malcolm Pease, and killing Sam. There was a huge turnout at St Faith's Crematorium for the funeral of this caring husband and father, who died a hero of the Norwich blitz.

The operators of the private air-raid spotting post at the base of their observation tower in Bracondale. This was funded by Boulton & Paul, Colmans and the North Eastern Railway Company. Back row, left to right: Fred Juby, Walter Buttifant, Albert Waterson, George Gray, Walter Abel. Front row: F. Pegg, Ernest West (Second Officer, Carrow Fire Brigade), Harry Rust (Chief Officer, CFB), Frank Harrison, Edwin Comber.

Bottlers, foremen and the manager of Steward & Patterson's Pockthorpe Brewery on Barrack Street, Norwich. Throughout the war they kept the supplies going to messes, NAAFIs and, in special parcels sent from home, to servicemen all over the world. Cheers!

Workers' playtime at Barnards Ltd, Salhouse Road, Norwich, *c.* 1942. In the centre aisle of the canteen 'theatre' are Jack Hulbert, his brother Claude and his wife Cecily Courtledge, with the works manager at the rear of the group. One lunchtime these entertainers called in for a short performance as they were appearing in the city that week. Barnards produced everything from wire mesh to Nissen huts for the war effort.

Ladies producing utility wear and uniforms at F.W. Harmer & Co. Ltd in St Andrew's Street. Even though the premises were damaged in the blitz these home front fighters, like so many others all too often forgotten, carried on doing what they could till the wreckage was cleared and work could commence again. In the event of an air raid, notices around the room direct workers to their group shelter.

The crew of B-24 Liberator 'Touch of Texas', the 389th Bomb Group, 8th US Army Air Force, Station No. 114, Hethel, 1943. The crew arrived in mid-June 1943 and flew Liberators on 321 missions, most in daylight. The 389th BG was credited with 7,579 sorties and dropped 17,548 tons of bombs on targets such as Berlin, Koblenz, Hamburg and Frankfurt. Having flown a number of successful missions, sadly the crew crashed after a raid at Easter 1944. Liberators became a familiar sight over Norfolk in formation or struggling back after a mission. East Anglia hosted thousands of American servicemen from aerodromes concentrated in the region. Good or bad, everyone from that time has memories of the 'Yanks', but we must never forget those boys who never returned 'State Side'.

Guildhall Hill, Norwich, late 1942. After the hell of April 1942 and its aftermath of emergency repairs and clearing up there were further raids, but the tide of the war was turning. Songs like 'It's a Lovely Day Tomorrow' were sung with greater fervour and the fine old city began to get back on its feet.

Civil Defence members in front of the Railway Hotel, Coltishall, *c.* 1942. This group is typical of the units of the Civil Defence organization found in every town, village and city across the country. These groups were also called upon in the capacity of auxiliary rescue parties during the large raids on the city.

Cowman Don Griffin and his prize bull at River Farm, Honing, 1941. Although he attempted to enlist he was not allowed to, as he was a 'key agricultural farm worker' and thus a 'reserved occupation'. His work and that of hundreds like him across the county was essential. Meat was rationed by price: adults to 1s 2d and children to 7d per week. Butchers had Meat Allocation Officers to distribute their supplies each week and faced stiff penalties if they slaughtered without a Ministry of Food licence.

A Land Army Girls' parade at Mannington Hall, *c*. 1942. The Women's Land Army Organization was formed in the autumn of 1938. The recruiting drive began during March 1940. The minimum age was eighteen and applicants were interviewed and enrolment completed after a medical examination. They also had to make a signed statement to the effect that they were willing to work anywhere in England, and then undertook a four-week training programme.

Daylight on 23 July 1942 reveals the devastation caused by a Dornier 217 to the High Street, Cromer. Several buildings received direct hits and well-known local businesses were reduced to rubble. Casualties stood at eleven dead and thirteen injured. This horrific scene was observed by two powerless fire watchers on top of the church tower.

Battle training on the cliffs at Cromer, 1942. After making a seaborne landing, troops storm a steep advance under live machine-gun, rifle and mortar fire. Such exercises were carried out in sealed-off areas for secrecy.

Staff officers and members of the entourage accompanying Sir James Grigg, Secretary of State for War, observe the battle exercise under a smoke screen, near Great Yarmouth, May 1943.

King George VI and Queen Elizabeth visit RAF Coltishall, 1943. They inspected, met and talked with the men, and presented a crest to the Commanding Officer of the Air/Sea Rescue Squadron.

PO Cecil Thomas Kingsborough Cody being chaired by members of his squadron on the way to the mess during the royal visit to Coltishall, 1943. Ten minutes before the scheduled arrival of the royal party the signal 'Enemy aircraft approaching' was received. This twenty-year-old Irish-born pilot secured his first enemy kill after this scramble. Describing his incredible encounter with the Ju88 to Their Majesties, he was warmly congratulated.

Saluting base in front of Cromer Church for the parade for Wings Week, Sunday 13 June 1943. From left to right: Reginald Fitzjohn (Lloyds Bank Manager), Dr R.B. Fawkes, Field Marshal Lord Ironside, Capt. Owen Tudor (Resident Naval Liaison Officer), Harry Mitchell (Chairman of UDC), King Peter of Yugoslavia, Major Gurney, Sir Thomas Cook, Lady Cook and their two children, Air Vice-Marshal R.P. Mills.

RAF personnel on special duties at Great Yarmouth. Working from temporary 'barracks' in the large seafront hotels, these men were involved in top secret operations in enemy deception and subterfuge. These ranged from setting up dummy airfields ('Q' sites) to manufacturing evidence of fictitious troop movements to back-up messages deliberately sent from Intelligence HQ at Bletchley Park, Buckinghamshire, to be received by German Intelligence during the build-up to D-Day.

Grog ration issue aboard HMS *Kellett*. This was one of the ten vessels in the 4th Minesweeping Flotilla operating from Great Yarmouth. Originally armed with a 4 in gun fore and a couple of Lewis guns, she was refitted with 12 pounders fore and aft, at Ipswich in 1942. The flotilla was usually escorted by a mine-disposal trawler, which destroyed swept mines with gunfire, and acoustic or moored sweeps were carried out as far away as the Dutch coast. In March 1943 a force of E-boats was engaged off Smith's Knoll, outside Yarmouth; one blew up and another was rammed. Later that year a force of thirty German boats set out from Ijmuiden to attack shipping convoys. However, they were turned away off Cromer by five motor torpedo boats and suffered heavy losses.

Crew 'E', Royal Observer Corps, Norwich, 1943. Back row, left to right: Peter Godfrey, 'Red' Redmain, 'Junior' Smith, 'Bill' Taylor, Pfob ('Bert'), George Millbank, Arthur Cox, 'Elder' Smith, George Gainsford, Joe 'Stalin' Spinks, ? Clarke. Middle row: Reggie Ray, Charles Thurston, Ronnie Hill, Phyllis Sparks, Mrs Crook, Margery Betty, Joy Hanley, Miss Mason, Daisy Whatley, Mrs 'Willie' Wilson, John Underhill, ? Hyde-Clarke, Frank Lake. Front row: Phil Cooper, 'Willie' Wilson, Vic Reeve, Bill Cocking, Frank Marais, 'Pop' Pordage DC, 'Rammy' Ramsbottom, Bill Kearsley, 'Mid' Middleton.

Dersingham Special Police Constables, November 1944. Back row, left to right: Playford, Wells, Mapus-Smith, Whisker, Chambers, Twite, Bird, Cross, Benstead. Front row: S.P.C. Taylor, S.P.C. Batterbee, P.C. Goldthorpe, Sgt. Keeler, Ch. Con. Capt. S.H. van Neck CVO, MC, Supt. Woodeson, S.P.C. Reynolds, P.C. Mitchell, Det. Con. Watts, S.P.S. Dunger.

Mundesley Coast Guard, *c.* 1943. Back row, left to right: Fred Rudrum, Victor Strong, Percy Watson, Howard Dawes, Harry Mason, Ted Wallace, Robert Rivett, Reggie Earl, Jimmy Clarke, John Shanahan, District Officer Bailey. Front row: Billy Clarke, Bertie Moston, Herbert Rudrum, Raymond Barker, Cecil Barker. On the night of 9 April 1945 at 2.00 a.m. Reggie Earl and Howard Dawes captured a lifeboat full of 'German' soldiers. In fact they were four Russians who had been pressed into the *Wehrmacht* and, though unarmed, were still wearing uniforms, plus ten Dutch. All of them had escaped from the German-occupied island of Texel in the North Sea off Holland.

Miss Doris Fitt playing a very fine Britannia in the tableau for The Royal Norfolk Regiment as part of the Norwich Salute the Soldier week, 10–17 June 1944. Her fortitude in the role was commended by the chairman of the committee: 'I am afraid it was a bit of an ordeal as the weather was not too kind. I am glad to know that you suffered no ill effects.'

The recently decorated Capt. David Jamieson inspects a parade of men of the depot at Britannia Barracks, Saturday 4 November 1944. He had been awarded the VC for his part in the crucial battle for the Orne Bridgehead, Grimsbosq, Normandy, on 7/8 August 1944. He is accompanied by Lt.-Col. J.E. Hewick (Dorset Regiment), who was the Commanding Officer of the barracks.

With the Nazi downfall in Europe secured, the home front forces were disbanded in November and December 1944. Seen here is the final group photograph of the Ambulance Women's Section, North Walsham St John Ambulance Brigade. The group was nicknamed 'the Pick 'Em Up Girls', having been sent out on numerous occasions to recover the crews of crashed aircraft and blitz victims.

Men of the 4th Battalion, Norfolk Home Guard, pictured at their formal stand-down on 3 December 1944. This picture was presented to all members of the company by their Commanding Officer Lt.-Col. Lord Hastings. Many of them were employed on his estate at Melton Constable Hall.

VE Day, Norwich, 8 May 1945. In the words of Churchill it was a day when '. . . we may allow ourselves a brief period of rejoicing'. American and British military police and Norwich city police lined the route for the victory march in front of massed crowds. 'Eyes right' and the salute is given by ladies from the Women's Auxiliary Air Force as they march past Norwich City Hall.

Indian Troops march up Guildhall Hill for the VE Parade, reminding us of the continuing conflict in the Far East. 'Victory in the Jungles' was two long months away, on 15 August 1945.

8th June, 1946

T I send this personal message to you and all other boys and girls at school. For you have shared in the hardships and dangers of a total war and you have shared no less in the triumph of the Allied Nations.

I know you will always feel proud to belong to a country which was capable of such supreme effort; proud, too, of parents and elder brothers and sisters who by their courage, endurance and enterprise brought victory. May these qualities be yours as you grow up and join in the common effort to establish among the nations of the world unity and peace.

George R.I.

A card presented to schoolchildren to commemorate the Allied victory and the end of the Second World War.

SECTION FOUR

Postwar Years and the End of an Era

Soldiers of the Recruit Training Battalion, The Royal Norfolk Regiment, put the newly issued FN FAL rifle through its paces, February 1958.

Back home from the Second World War: returned servicemen and members of the welcome home committee from the village of Scottow, 1946. They are pictured outside the Oddfellows Hall, where they were treated to a fine dinner and each presented with £13 10s. Back row, left to right: D. Bell, C. Buck, W. Atkins, C. Hall, A. Tipple, G. Newstead, R. Rump, J. Watson, H. Roberts, C. Self, G. Fiddy, L. Rump, C. Atkins, R. Gray, I. Self, G. Cook, S. Wilson, N. Appleton. Front row: Mrs Pike, Mike Adams, P. Bowers, A. Alford, T. Buck, F. Newstead, J. Newstead, Miss J. Cutting.

A parade of The Royal Norfolk Regiment in front of City Hall, 3 October 1945. Representatives of every battalion paraded for the formal presentation of '. . . the privilege, honour and distinction of marching through the City on all ceremonial occasions with bayonets fixed, colours flying and bands playing'. This was conferred on the regiment by the City Council as a mark of affection and admiration of gallantry displayed by the regiment over nearly three hundred years.

The Operations Room of Norwich (No. 6 Group) Royal Observer Corps at Old Catton, 1949. This was a hive of activity, especially when there were fears of nuclear war. The corps carried out many exercises in monitoring and responding to such attacks, as well as coordinating the observation and tracking of aircraft. Under the operation codename 'Pheno' it even located and estimated the height of any unidentified flying objects.

RSM J.A. Sewell of the 4th Battalion, The Royal Norfolk Regiment (TA), inspects some of the scarlet tunics received at the Cattle Market Drill Hall, Norwich. They were sent in response to an advertisement placed in the *Eastern Daily Press* requesting such attire to equip the battalion band for the special parades in coronation year, 1952.

RSM W. Paskell details train parties from the 4th Battalion, The Royal Norfolk Regiment (TA), at Thorpe station, on their way to summer camp at Shorncliffe for two weeks, 1954.

National Servicemen of No. 9 (Randle) Platoon, The Royal Norfolk Regiment, December 1951. Back row, left to right: Ptes. Segon, Brown, Cook, Sheppard, Baldwin, Davies, Buswell, White, Harwood. Third row: Milne, Webber, Waters, Collins, Snelling, Last, Miller, Barham, Simper, Brown. Second row: Kindleysides, Powles, Woods, Balaam, Cock, Thurtle, Adams, Johnson, Bilner, Snell, Fenn. Front row: Howard, King, Sgt. Browne, 2nd Lt. Nelson, Cpl. Fox, Ptes. Brown and Thaxter. Most of these men went on to serve in Korea.

The last great homecoming parade in the county was held on 15 December 1954, when the soldiers of the 1st Battalion, The Royal Norfolk Regiment (many of them National Servicemen), returned from Hong Kong after fighting the war in Korea. As they march past City Hall with fixed bayonets and drawn swords, the salute is taken by Her Majesty's Lieutenant for Norfolk, Lt.-Col. Sir Edmund Bacon, Bt, OBE, TD. They proceeded to the cathedral and afterwards a fine dinner was held in the Samson and Hercules.

Farewell to the Regimental Flag, 29 August 1959. Owing to the government's recommended reductions in the British Army a number of infantry regiments were to be amalgamated, among them The Royal Norfolk Regiment. This came as a bitter blow after almost three hundred years of distinguished service. The closing service was held at Britannia Barracks, after which the retreat was sounded and the Regimental Flag was lowered for the last time.

Norwich Cemetery, Military Section. The Cross of Sacrifice denotes this special Commonwealth War Graves Commission cemetery. Soldiers, sailors and airmen from Norfolk killed in theatres of war all over the world have been returned to their home soil to rest. They lie side by side with servicemen from New Zealand, Australia, Canada and Poland who were killed around the county. Even buried here are German airmen who were killed over the county and German sailors washed up on our shores. War has no favour; lives are lost on both sides. Here lie friend and foe, together in eternal peace. In the words of Lawrence Binyon, in his poem 'For the Fallen' written in September 1914:

> They shall grow not old, as we that are left grow old;
> Age shall not weary them, nor the years condemn.
> At the going down of the sun and in the morning
> We will remember them.

Acknowledgements

I should like to express my sincere gratitude to the following without whose contribution, knowledge and time this book would not have been possible:

Tony Williamson • Terry Davy • Harry Barnard • Percy Trett • Peter Brooks
Joan Banger • Eric Reading • Sqn. Ldr. J. Love • Bridgette Yates • John Nockells
Judy Ball • Bob Collis (Norfolk and Suffolk Aviation Museum)
Basil Gowen • Brian Brown • Ivor Self • Frederick Mace AMPS • Brian Veriod
Alan Womack • Norwich Central and Great Yarmouth Libraries (Local
Studies) • Norfolk Museums Service • Maritime Museum for East Anglia
Norfolk Rural Life Museum • USAF Second Air Division Memorial Library
Eastern Counties Newspapers (Derek James, Neville Miller and ECN Library
Staff) • Imperial War Museum • Trustees of the Royal Norfolk Regimental
Museum • the Pulham Market Society (Jocelyn Rawlence) • Cromer Lifeboat
Museum • Norfolk Constabulary • Terry Burchell for photographic wonders.

Special thanks to my family for their endless support and encouragement to this temperamental author.

Finally thanks to the many people too numerous to mention from over the years who have donated to, inspired and helped me in my collecting and research.

BRITAIN IN OLD PHOTOGRAPHS

ALDERNEY

Alderney: A Second Selection, *B Bonnard*

BEDFORDSHIRE

Bedfordshire at Work, *N Lutt*

BERKSHIRE

Maidenhead, *M Hayles & D Hedges*
Around Maidenhead, *M Hayles & B Hedges*
Reading, *P Southerton*
Reading: A Second Selection, *P Southerton*
Sandhurst and Crowthorne, *K Dancy*
Around Slough, *J Hunter & K Hunter*
Around Thatcham, *P Allen*
Around Windsor, *B Hedges*

BUCKINGHAMSHIRE

Buckingham and District, *R Cook*
High Wycombe, *R Goodearl*
Around Stony Stratford, *A Lambert*

CHESHIRE

Cheshire Railways, *M Hitches*
Chester, *S Nichols*

CLWYD

Clwyd Railways, *M Hitches*

CLYDESDALE

Clydesdale, *Lesmahagow Parish Historical Association*

CORNWALL

Cornish Coast, *T Bowden*
Falmouth, *P Gilson*
Lower Fal, *P Gilson*
Around Padstow, *M McCarthy*
Around Penzance, *J Holmes*
Penzance and Newlyn, *J Holmes*
Around Truro, *A Lyne*
Upper Fal, *P Gilson*

CUMBERLAND

Cockermouth and District, *J Bernard Bradbury*
Keswick and the Central Lakes, *J Marsh*
Around Penrith, *F Boyd*
Around Whitehaven, *H Fancy*

DERBYSHIRE

Derby, *D Buxton*
Around Matlock, *D Barton*

DEVON

Colyton and Seaton, *T Gosling*
Dawlish and Teignmouth, *G Gosling*
Devon Aerodromes, *K Saunders*
Exeter, *P Thomas*
Exmouth and Budleigh Salterton, *T Gosling*
From Haldon to Mid-Dartmoor, *T Hall*
Honiton and the Otter Valley, *J Yallop*
Around Kingsbridge, *K Tanner*
Around Seaton and Sidmouth, *T Gosling*
Seaton, Axminster and Lyme Regis, *T Gosling*

DORSET

Around Blandford Forum, *B Cox*
Bournemouth, *M Colman*
Bridport and the Bride Valley, *J Burrell & S Humphries*
Dorchester, *T Gosling*
Around Gillingham, *P Crocker*

DURHAM

Darlington, *G Flynn*
Darlington: A Second Selection, *G Flynn*
Durham People, *M Richardson*
Houghton-le-Spring and Hetton-le-Hole, *K Richardson*
Houghton-le-Spring and Hetton-le-Hole:
    A Second Selection, *K Richardson*
Sunderland, *S Miller & B Bell*
Teesdale, *D Coggins*
Teesdale: A Second Selection, *P Raine*
Weardale, *J Crosby*
Weardale: A Second Selection, *J Crosby*

DYFED

Aberystwyth and North Ceredigion,
    Dyfed Cultural Services Dept
Haverfordwest, *Dyfed Cultural Services Dept*
Upper Tywi Valley, *Dyfed Cultural Services Dept*

ESSEX

Around Grays, *B Evans*

GLOUCESTERSHIRE

Along the Avon from Stratford to Tewkesbury, *J Jeremiah*
Cheltenham: A Second Selection, *R Whiting*
Cheltenham at War, *P Gill*
Cirencester, *J Welsford*
Around Cirencester, *E Cuss & P Griffiths*
Forest, The, *D Mullin*
Gloucester, *J Voyce*
Around Gloucester, *A Sutton*
Gloucester: From the Walwin Collection, *J Voyce*
North Cotswolds, *D Viner*
Severn Vale, *A Sutton*
Stonehouse to Painswick, *A Sutton*
Stroud and the Five Valleys, *S Gardiner & L Padin*
Stroud and the Five Valleys: A Second Selection,
    S Gardiner & L Padin
Stroud's Golden Valley, *S Gardiner & L Padin*
Stroudwater and Thames & Severn Canals,
    E Cuss & S Gardiner
Stroudwater and Thames & Severn Canals: A Second
    Selection, *E Cuss & S Gardiner*
Tewkesbury and the Vale of Gloucester, *C Hilton*
Thornbury to Berkeley, *J Hudson*
Uley, Dursley and Cam, *A Sutton*
Wotton-under-Edge to Chipping Sodbury, *A Sutton*

GWYNEDD

Anglesey, *M Hitches*
Gwynedd Railways, *M Hitches*
Around Llandudno, *M Hitches*
Vale of Conwy, *M Hitches*

HAMPSHIRE

Gosport, *J Sadden*
Portsmouth, *P Rogers & D Francis*

HEREFORDSHIRE

Herefordshire, *A Sandford*

HERTFORDSHIRE

Barnet, *I Norrie*
Hitchin, *A Fleck*
St Albans, *S Mullins*
Stevenage, *M Appleton*

ISLE OF MAN

The Tourist Trophy, *B Snelling*

ISLE OF WIGHT

Newport, *D Parr*
Around Ryde, *D Parr*

JERSEY

Jersey: A Third Selection, *R Lemprière*

KENT

Bexley, *M Scott*
Broadstairs and St Peter's, *J Whyman*
Bromley, Keston and Hayes, *M Scott*
Canterbury: A Second Selection, *D Butler*
Chatham and Gillingham, *P MacDougall*
Chatham Dockyard, *P MacDougall*
Deal, *J Broady*
Early Broadstairs and St Peter's, *B Wootton*
East Kent at War, *D Collyer*
Eltham, *J Kennett*
Folkestone: A Second Selection, *A Taylor & E Rooney*
Goudhurst to Tenterden, *A Guilmant*
Gravesend, *R Hiscock*
Around Gravesham, *R Hiscock & D Grierson*
Herne Bay, *J Hawkins*
Lympne Airport, *D Collyer*
Maidstone, *I Hales*
Margate, *R Clements*
RAF Hawkinge, *R Humphreys*
RAF Manston, *RAF Manston History Club*
RAF Manston: A Second Selection,
    RAF Manston History Club
Ramsgate and Thanet Life, *D Perkins*
Romney Marsh, *E Carpenter*
Sandwich, *C Wanostrocht*
Around Tonbridge, *C Bell*
Tunbridge Wells, *M Rowlands & I Beavis*
Tunbridge Wells: A Second Selection,
    M Rowlands & I Beavis
Around Whitstable, *C Court*
Wingham, Adisham and Littlebourne, *M Crane*

LANCASHIRE

Around Barrow-in-Furness, *J Garbutt & J Marsh*
Blackpool, *C Rothwell*
Bury, *J Hudson*
Chorley and District, *J Smith*
Fleetwood, *C Rothwell*
Heywood, *J Hudson*
Around Kirkham, *C Rothwell*
Lancashire North of the Sands, *J Garbutt & J Marsh*
Around Lancaster, *S Ashworth*
Lytham St Anne's, *C Rothwell*
North Fylde, *C Rothwell*
Radcliffe, *J Hudson*
Rossendale, *B Moore & N Dunnachie*

LEICESTERSHIRE

Around Ashby-de-la-Zouch, *K Hillier*
Charnwood Forest, *I Keil, W Humphrey & D Wix*
Leicester, *D Burton*
Leicester: A Second Selection, *D Burton*
Melton Mowbray, *T Hickman*
Around Melton Mowbray, *T Hickman*
River Soar, *D Wix, P Shacklock & I Keil*
Rutland, *T Clough*
Vale of Belvoir, *T Hickman*
Around the Welland Valley, *S Mastoris*

LINCOLNSHIRE

Grimsby, *J Tierney*
Around Grimsby, *J Tierney*
Grimsby Docks, *J Tierney*
Lincoln, *D Cuppleditch*